THE HYPNOTIC LANGUAGE OF SUCCESS

DR. MARITSA YZAGUIRRE-KELLEY

The Hypnotic Language of Success

Dr. Maritsa Yzaguirre-Kelley

The Hypnotic Language of Success

Copyright © 2017 by Maritsa Yzaguirre-Kelley

This book is not intended as a substitute for the medical advice of physicians. The reader should regularly consult a physician in matters relating to his/her health and particularly with respect to any symptoms which may require diagnosis or medical attention.

Printed in the United States of America
First Printing, 2017
Formatted by LC Taylor Publishings
Cover Design by LC Taylor Publishings
www.lctaylorpublishings.com

Table of Contents

Introduction: The Hypnotic Language

The art of language is so hypnotic that most of us dismiss its hypnotic spell. You've been hypnotized. You are under my spell. You aren't just under my spell. You are under the spell of any one and anything that you allow in your presence.

What does that mean? It means you are in a trance living as if you are, but never present. Can you imagine how scary it would be if you allowed your mind to be in the wrong space. Can you imagine the effects if you had your mind in the right space? I can.

I remember, it was October 2nd, 2012. It doesn't seem that long ago, but it was a lifetime ago. I decided that everything was just wrong. I wasn't even sure which way was up. I needed something new, something different, something real.

My son, dad, and I hopped on a plan to Puerto Rico – one of my favorite places to visit. I woke up early every day went to the gym, where I enjoyed running. I spent much of the rest of the day in a deep meditative state, I thought of things I wanted or needed, and then I created a plan.

Chapter 1: You're in a Trance

Whether you realize it or not, we are subjected to messages every day without realizing. We hear messages about how we should act, dress, or what we should buy for dinner. The media, as well as the fashion industry, have learned how to take cues to ensure society strives to achieve a certain level of success and achievement. Over the long term. people are seeing and consuming material that was engrained into their subconscious.

There are many methods that are notorious for allowing the bad information, as well as the negative programming, to slip in. Think about it – have you ever fallen asleep after reading something or watching something on television and end up having the weirdest dream?

It's because we are being hypnotized by everything around us.

Techniques Used for Brain Washing in Every Day Interactions

✓ Repeat the same slogans repetitively!

Whether you realize it or not you are bombarded with the same material repeatedly. This means whatever you're hearing is becoming a part of your subconscious mind. If you think about it, when you are hearing messages over the radio, or you're hearing some other context, it is important to know what you are hearing.

It might be as simple as a campaign slogan, but when something is repeated, it is designed to slip into your subconscious in a way that will ensure you are going to remember the slogan.

In the same way that a mantra can calm you, and can become a source of information, this allows information into the brain without being completely filtered.

✓ Isolation from Others

If you attend a camp, or you attend a church, you will find that one-way people can have influence is by removing you from their crowd. You should make sure you are always part of a large crowd/group to avoid possible influence.

If you are a part of a company or group, they may want you to complete a training or a conversion, that will ensure they are able to make agreements with you in isolation. When you are in a group like, there may be a suggestion to not take drugs, skip eating, or smoking to have an effect of conversion. One of the complex parts of this the change that takes place within the internal nervous system which ensures that there will be conversion.

It's important to recognize what can happen in the moment that allows you to be programmed by this kind of influence and this kind of state. There are many ways to keep yourself from being brain washed, but you need to recognize the likely symptoms.

✓ If You Imitate People, They Will Give You Things!

Ensure that people like you. This technique is used with many people – such as servers. Repeated words which work to make sure you can get people to like you as well as know your influence.

This is the same method that servers and bartenders use to imitate the language as well as the concerns of the guests allowing them to forge a special connection.

✓ Juxtapose "Don't" Instead of "Can't"

When it comes to dieting there are many people who are on the border of what is craved and what is actually needed to survive. What this means is you want to make sure you are not focusing on the things that people cannot do, but instead what they do not want to do.

If you look at the diet industry, you will see that there are many things happening on a regular basis that ensures you are messing with the diet of someone who is trying to lose weight by saying that obesity is a disease.

So, if a dieter is going to look at the perspective of what they don't want to do versus seeing it as a restriction they will then see it as a method of empowerment vs restriction.

That means that it is possible to ensure that you are going to have access to the best ideas by simply allowing the client to say they don't want something vs. they can't do something…it adds that level of empowerment.

✓ Using a Ritual to Increase Satisfaction.

Humanity rituals are markers of significance, which means adding a little ritual to the process will make things more special. There have been many studies done that indicate that doing something as simple as saying Abracadabra above the food will make it taste better. Advertising campaigns that add any kind of ritual to the process ensure that there is a greater appeal.

✓ Say I am Excited!

If you find yourself in a difficult position and you are trying to rewire the situation to get beyond a large challenge the secret is to make sure that you are saying that you are excited. That means that you want to focus on all the positives that are a part of the world and the situation so that you are going to look the challenge in the eye and laugh at it.

✓ A Jedi Mind Trick of Reason

If you give someone a reason, they will likely allow amends to whatever the situation is, as well as make all kinds of changes to the protocol and the way they do things. That means it is possible for people to get away with much more if they give you a reason.

If someone tells you for example why he or she needs to get in front of you, you are likely going to allow them to do so simply because they have given you a reason. This is one of the oldest Jedi mind tricks in the book and remains a reason that there are many people who employ it daily.

There is no way around seeing hypnosis in daily life, but it does mean that there are many ways that you can decide to wake up and take your life back!

Chapter 2: Break Unwanted Hypnosis

We are all told that there are certain things we cannot do, that there is no way that we can have it all. Within some instances this is true…there are limits to what happens with the body and with space and time. However, it is very important to make sure that you know that you can have the life you want as well as make sure that you are able to have what you have looked for your entire life.

There are many people who tell us that it is impossible to do X because of X reason… but at the end of the day, if you look at some of the greatest entrepreneurs in history you will see that it is possible to restart your life and to take it back at any moment whenever you want to.

There are many people who have done just that at any point in their lives and have turned things around by deciding that they did not believe the language and the lies that they were being fed by the rest of the world.

It was a moment of decision that made all the difference and ensured that there was going to be another way to turn the tide as well as to change everything with the simplest concrete decision.

Every person at any moment in time had the ability to make that decision and just had to take control of their lives but there are very few people who are ready to make that decision. A few examples of people who have done what they wanted and gotten everything in return.

Oprah: Fired from her television station in Chicago because she was not able to get the ratings which suggested she could rise to the top of the female earners and achieve the ultimate success as an author, host, and network owner. She is a mogul and a force within herself that has continued to show that anything is possible with enough determination.

Steve Jobs: Fired from the company that he had created, Steve decided to reinvent himself and take real action. Steve was one of those people who came from a blue-collar family and who should have statistically never risen to success.

Andrew Carnegie: Started working on a railroad and had no education. He worked his way from laying railroad tracks to becoming one of the largest tycoons in business overnight with a few simple planned moves.

Many of these people had no idea that they were not going to be able to do what it what that they wanted to do and there is the secret to their success. Not having anyone tell them that they couldn't do something means that they were able to do it.

The reason that they could is because there was no programming saying that it was going to be impossible to execute whatever their dream or their vision was. Without knowing that something was impossible it was possible for them to achieve what others thought was not.

Chapter 3: Watch Your Mouth

You may have heard the old cliché that 'words have power'. Well it is very true. It is important to use them and to make sure that you understand the power that is associated with each word. Maybe you are familiar with the words, "The Lord Created the Word, and the word was God."

Whether or not you are religious, you will see that there are some very specific things that must be looked at when you have a vibration of words or sounds you will see that there is real meaning to them.

When you look at words throughout the ancient books you will see tons of references to creation happening from the words that are used. The reason that this happens is that you can boldly use tools that will allow you to create your reality around you by the words you use.

The effects of what you are trying to manifest and the things that you are trying to do in your life are all based on the way that you look at the situation. There is real power in your words and it's important to realize that they are an affirmation or confirmation of how people think about themselves or others.

It is important to see that these are a part of the way that reality happens. That means that it has never been more important than to make sure that you are not using one of your most important assets in a bad way.

✓   The Power of Words

When it comes to being normal, you may not think about the way your words impact you or the way that they allow you to talk about your situation or your issues. You will see that there are many ways that people look at events as well as situations and they are not able to have access to any ways to look at their situation.

This means you need to make sure that you are looking at your situation and you are looking at the words that you are manifesting in your life. If you are telling yourself that you are going to be unlucky in love, in work or in other situations you need to see that you need to know what you are complaining about and why.

You need to know how you are creating the life that you are living as well. What that means is that you need to make sure that you know the words that you are using and that you are thinking about them before you make mistakes.

When there is an improved self-awareness it means that you are going to be able to remove many of the negative words like can't, shouldn't, won't and many more that will allow you to then manifest the life that you want to when you have removed you negative programming.

Chapter 4: Learning a New Language

When it comes to learning a language one of the most important things that you must do is realize what you have been doing wrong. A large part of that is knowing and finding what have been your limiting moves and your limiting choices of language over the course of the past few years or maybe your whole life.

✓ Limiting Your Negative Thoughts

When it comes to thinking, one thing that may not be clear to you is that your negative thoughts are directly affecting your reality. You need to make sure you are getting rid of negativity, instead of letting it sink into your soul. This could be done with changing your language or similar tactics. You want to think about how you can change it in the moment and then you will be able to purge them from your experience once and for all. Here are a few suggestions.

❖ Change Your Position and Your Movement

You want to look at how you are standing and see if you are slouching as well as make sure that you are looking at how you are reacting to others. You need to make sure that you are standing up straight and smiling.

You want to make sure that you are also standing in an open and not closed body stance so that you are going to change your ideas about how you are thinking.

❖ Talk Through Your Situation

When you experience negative thoughts, this can be because of things that you need to be able to get out of your system and you have not found the right way to process them. You want to make sure that you are going to look at the issue and you need the ideas and the thoughts of someone else.

When you can bounce your ideas off someone else you will be able to see what the issue is and will be able to likely form a plan that is going to let you turn that negativity around.

❖ Spend a Moment and Calm Your Mind

Think about taking a quiet moment in the day and making sure that you can calm your stress and your negativity with a moment of perspective. You want to make sure that you are looking at everything that is going on around you and looking at the mindset so that you are going to be able to know how you can find solutions.

You will see that there is usually a positive spin on the situation. You want to make sure that you can look at all the thinking patterns.

❖ Change Your Tone

One thing that is very important is to make sure that you are going to be able to pull yourself out of a difficult time and that means that you need to look at your situation as finding solutions instead of speaking a language of being a victim. You want to make sure that you are always able to put a positive spin on any situation and you will be very happy with the response.

✿ Be Very Creative

When you have a negative thought, one of the best ways to get it out is to make sure that you can turn around your perspective so that you are going to be able to look at your thoughts and create something that is going to be of value of your pain.

You need to get your thoughts out in a way that is going to be meaningful and allow you to clear your system. You want to make sure that you can think about something that is a negative and turn it into a positive and look at the long-term art you can create. Whether your media is poetry or something else you will see all that you need to make sure that you are going to get that emotion out and that you are ready to really feel better.

✿ Get Out in Nature

There is a reason the Japanese make sure to get out and have time in nature. You will see that there are many ways to make sure that you are able to turn your situation around and that means that you want to turn your time around and think about what you are grateful for.

❖ List All You're Thankful For

If you are having a negative moment and you are full of negative thoughts take a moment and simply list what you are grateful for and you will be able to have a moment to understand what you need to be happy for in the moment.

Chapter 5: Speaking & Thinking in Terms of Empowerment

When it comes to making sure you are going to be successful at turning your goals into realities and achieving the success you have been looking for you need to use empowering language. Sit back and think for a moment about all the language that you use on a regular basis that it is going to be empowering for you.

Think about what language can do....it can help you be a success or a failure, and control the way that you think about yourself. You need to know that when you speak yourself into more successful and empowering language that you are going to be able to take things to the next level and that means that you are going to see a new rise in your success and your station.

Here are a few things to consider:

<u>Use the Best Words</u>:

When you are speaking you need to make sure that you are using the right words and that means that you want to make sure that you know the context. Never say that you cannot do something. Think again about how to turn the words into the reality that you are looking for and for the emotions that are behind those words.

<u>Use Your Words with Meaning:</u>

When you are speaking to someone it is important to make sure that you are using the right words and that means that you want to be able to offer a real yes or no answer. You will find that you are able to really paint yourself as someone of your word and that others will respect you and will value all you have to say in this circumstance.

<u>Know When You Are Going to Speak:</u>

You want to make sure that you are taking the time to know when you want to speak. Sometimes you need to be silent and that means that you do not need to speak in the moment when it is uncalled for. That is one of the most difficult lessons and means that you need to see that you can be very empowering with your speech.

When speaking to yourself, you need to use correct language, as well as when you are speaking to others. You are going to build a new self that is built on empowerment as well as manifesting what you want.

After Thought

Success is something always within your reach, if you are willing to reprogram yourself with the right influences and words. There is nothing that you cannot achieve when you have looked at yourself and have realized where you are and what it will take to get you where you want to be.

Whether it is the limiting language, the limiting beliefs, or the general negativity in your life there is a way out with a simple shift in the script. Take the time to let the words that we have just gone through here sink in and decide how you want things to be different. You are after all just a few actions and thoughts away. Manifest the hypnotic language of success.

About the Author

May name is Maritsa Yzaguirre-Kelley. I started out with a Masters in Mental Health Counseling and I went to work for one of the largest drug and alcohol treatment centers in the country as their Executive director. I hold certificates in Alternative Medicine, Clinical Hypnosis, and NLP. I went on to complete my doctorate in counseling as well.

My motivation for starting my coaching/consultation company, was so I can help professionals whose work has over taken their lives, break free and live.

I focus on teaching clients to live a life that is a balance between a sound mind and a sound body. My methods are revolutionary, as I blend the techniques of NLP, hypnotism, and other alternative methods, such as yoga.

I call South Florida my home even though I was born in Massachusetts. I have 2 boys, 3 dogs, and of course my amazing husband. We enjoy playing golf, going to the beach, gym, and playing with the kids. If I was still working in corporate being able to have that quality time to do the things I enjoy with the people I love would be unheard of.

For more information

Visit:
http://www.maximizewithrits.com
Or Email: Rits@Maximizewithrits.com

Click here and Sign Up for my **NEWSLETTER** to receive News & Updates!